★ ALWAYS ★
Grateful

A GUIDED JOURNAL
for *Everyday* GRATITUDE

JENNIFER LEIGHT

galison

www.galison.com f◘ @galisongift
70 West 36th Street, 11th Floor
New York, NY 10018

Design by Katie Jennings Campbell
Embroidery by Walker Boyes

Images used under license from Shutterstock.com

ISBN: 978-0-7353-5505-7

First Edition: December 2017

Designed and printed in the United States of America.

10 9 8 7 6 5 4 3 2 1

This journal belongs to:

_____

When it comes to life
the critical thing is
whether you take things
for granted or take
them with gratitude.

—G. K. CHESTERTON

In the pursuit of health and happiness,

we often overlook the power of gratitude in our everyday lives. It's so simple, yet so life-changing. In fact, gratitude has been proven to:

* IMPROVE RELATIONSHIPS
* LESSEN ACHES AND PAINS AND PROMOTE OVERALL HEALTH
* BRING ON BETTER SLEEP
* BOOST SELF–ESTEEM
* REDUCE STRESS

Living with gratitude just makes you feel amazing in body, mind, and soul! The trick: making it an everyday practice. That's where *Always Grateful* comes in. Each page brings you inspiration to fill your days with gratitude and simple paths to express it. Spend even a few minutes with this journal each day and you will feel burdens lifted and blessings overflowing.

AT TIMES OUR
OWN LIGHT GOES OUT
AND IS REKINDLED
BY A SPARK FROM
ANOTHER PERSON.
EACH OF US HAS CAUSE
TO THINK WITH DEEP
GRATITUDE OF THOSE
WHO HAVE LIGHTED THE
FLAME WITHIN US.

—ALBERT SCHWEITZER

Who are you grateful for

AS A GUIDE OUT OF TIMES OF DARKNESS?

FEELING GRATITUDE

and not expressing it is like

WRAPPING A PRESENT

and not giving it.

—WILLIAM ARTHUR WARD

MISSED A CHANCE TO SHARE GRATITUDE?

Actually, it's never too late. Reach out to someone you meant to thank through a note or call. Lost track of the connection? Share your thoughts here—you'll still benefit from putting your gratitude into words.

_____

_____

_____

_____

_____

_____

_____

_____

_____

_____

_____

_____

_____

WHAT MIRACLES HAVE YOU EXPERIENCED TODAY?

_____

_____

_____

_____

_____

_____

_____

_____

_____

_____

_____

_____

_____

_____

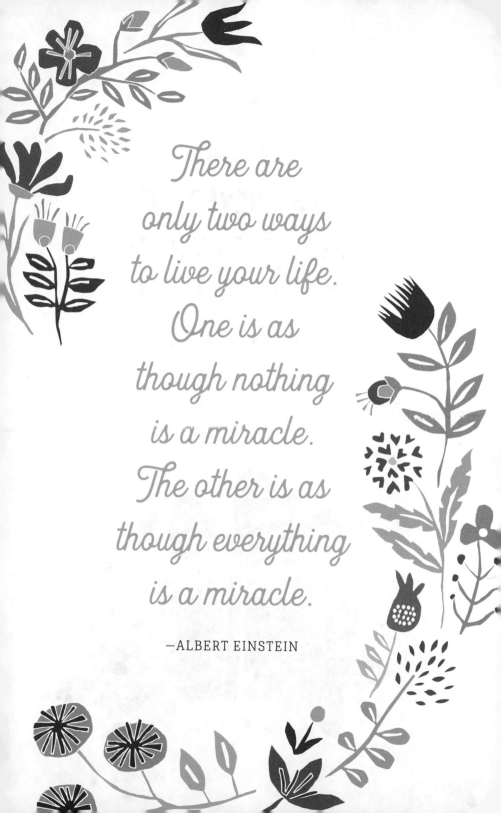

There are
only two ways
to live your life.
One is as
though nothing
is a miracle.
The other is as
though everything
is a miracle.

—ALBERT EINSTEIN

As we express
our gratitude,

WE MUST NEVER FORGET
THAT THE HIGHEST
APPRECIATION IS NOT
TO UTTER WORDS,

but to live by them.

—JOHN F. KENNEDY

How will you live out
YOUR GRATITUDE TODAY?

_____

_____

_____

_____

_____

_____

_____

_____

_____

_____

_____

_____

_____

_____

_____

_____

GRATITUDE IS THE HEALTHIEST OF ALL HUMAN EMOTIONS.

THE MORE YOU EXPRESS GRATITUDE FOR WHAT YOU HAVE, THE MORE LIKELY YOU WILL HAVE EVEN MORE TO EXPRESS GRATITUDE FOR.

—ZIG ZIGLAR

What negative emotions does gratitude help you overcome?

Gratitude

CHANGES
THE PANGS
OF MEMORY
INTO A
TRANQUIL JOY.

—DIETRICH BONHOEFFER

What challenging time from the past can you now see in a new light, thanks to gratitude for what the present holds?

_____

_____

_____

_____

_____

_____

_____

_____

_____

_____

_____

_____

_____

_____

_____

_____

WHAT SPECIAL TRAITS OR TALENTS DO YOU CARRY? TAKE A MOMENT TO FEEL GRATITUDE FOR THEM AND HOW THEY MAKE YOU *YOU*.

*We do not need magic
to change the world.
We carry all the power we
need inside ourselves
already.*

—J. K. ROWLING

IT'S THE JOY AND CHALLENGE OF LOOKING AT THE WORLD WITH CHILDLIKE EYES— EAGER TO CAPTURE WHATEVER IS IN FRONT OF THEM.

—STANLEY HAINSWORTH

Take a gratitude walk and record all the blessings you experience—the aroma from a bakery, the sun's warmth on your skin, the sounds of children playing and laughing.

Gratitude is riches.

Complaint is poverty.

—DORIS DAY

WHAT COMPLAINTS WILL YOU DROP
IN FAVOR OF GRATITUDE TODAY?

Does not the gratitude of the dog put to shame any man who is ungrateful to his benefactors?

—SAINT BASIL

LOOK AT YOUR LIFE THROUGH A DOG'S EYES.

What simple care and comforts do you have to be grateful for?

Gratitude helps you to grow and expand; GRATITUDE BRINGS JOY AND LAUGHTER INTO YOUR LIFE AND INTO THE LIVES OF ALL THOSE AROUND YOU.

—EILEEN CADDY

How does your gratitude touch the lives of others?

WHEN WAS THE LAST "BAD DAY" YOU HAD? HOW COULD GRATITUDE HAVE CHANGED IT?

_____

_____

_____

_____

_____

_____

_____

_____

_____

_____

_____

_____

_____

_____

_____

At the age of 18,
I made up my mind
to never have another
bad day in my life.
I dove into an endless sea
of gratitude from which
I've never emerged.

—PATCH ADAMS

Three meals plus bedtime make four sure blessings a day.

—MASON COOLEY

WHOM CAN YOU MAKE A MEAL FOR
OR INVITE OUT TO DINNER?

In what situations are you tempted to give away your contentment, joy, gratitude, and peace? How can you guard against that?

_____

_____

_____

_____

_____

_____

_____

_____

_____

_____

_____

_____

_____

_____

_____

_____

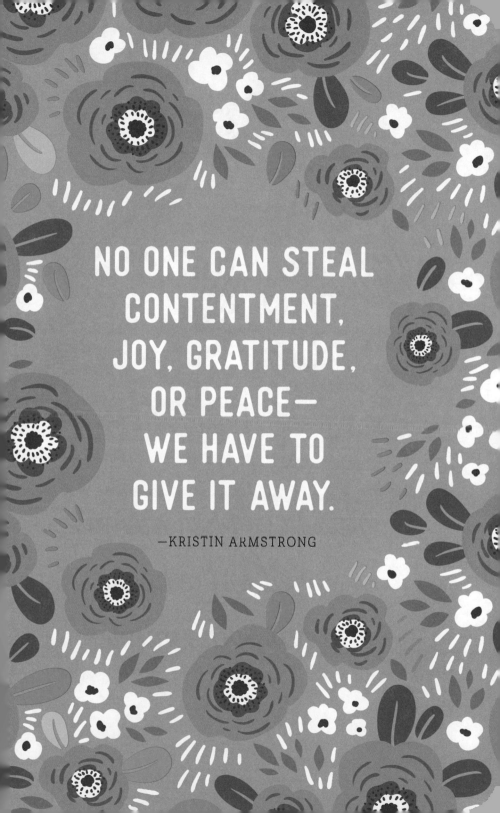

NO ONE CAN STEAL
CONTENTMENT,
JOY, GRATITUDE,
OR PEACE—
WE HAVE TO
GIVE IT AWAY.

—KRISTIN ARMSTRONG

Gratitude is when memory
is stored in the heart
and not in the mind.

—LIONEL HAMPTON

IN WHAT AREAS OF YOUR LIFE CAN YOU LET YOUR HEART LEAD A LITTLE MORE?

LOOK AT THE SKY:
THAT IS FOR YOU.
REMEMBER THIS
WHEN YOU WAKE UP
IN THE MORNING
AND THINK YOU
HAVE NOTHING.

—MIRANDA JULY

The world holds natural gifts all around us.

WHERE CAN YOU LOOK IN NATURE FOR SIGNS OF HOPE?

IT'S A SIGN
OF MEDIOCRITY
WHEN YOU
DEMONSTRATE
GRATITUDE WITH
MODERATION.

—ROBERTO BENIGNI

Whom can you shower with gratitude?
HOW WILL YOU DO IT?

WHOM CAN YOU MODEL GRATITUDE FOR?
HOW WILL YOU DO IT?

*When a person
doesn't have gratitude,
something is missing
in his or her humanity.*

—ELIE WIESEL

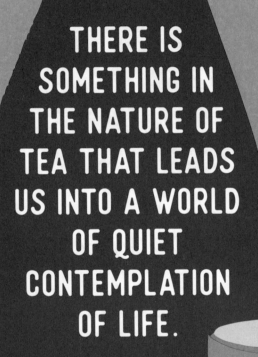

THERE IS
SOMETHING IN
THE NATURE OF
TEA THAT LEADS
US INTO A WORLD
OF QUIET
CONTEMPLATION
OF LIFE.

—LIN YUTANG

Try devoting your tea or coffee time to focusing on gratitude. With each sip, write down a simple pleasure for which you are thankful.

_____

_____

_____

_____

_____

_____

_____

_____

_____

_____

_____

_____

_____

_____

_____

Let us swell with gratitude
and allow it to overwhelm us.

—GRACE GEALEY

WHEN WAS THE LAST TIME YOU FELT OVERWHELMED BY GRATITUDE?

DESCRIBE THE EMOTIONS.

IF YOU WERE
TO ASK ME TO SUM UP
MY LIFE IN ONE WORD,

gratitude

—CAROLE KING

What words sum up your life as you've lived it so far?

AS YOU WANT TO LIVE IT?

Silent gratitude

ISN'T VERY MUCH
TO ANYONE.

—GERTRUDE STEIN

What habits and practices can you adopt to help you remember to express your gratitude?

_____

_____

_____

_____

_____

_____

_____

_____

_____

_____

_____

_____

_____

_____

_____

_____

LET US BE GRATEFUL TO PEOPLE WHO MAKE US HAPPY; THEY ARE THE CHARMING GARDENERS WHO MAKE OUR SOULS BLOSSOM.

—MARCEL PROUST

Whom can you spend more time with, to bring more joy and
gratefulness into your life?

_____

_____

_____

_____

_____

_____

_____

_____

_____

_____

_____

_____

_____

_____

_____

Fill the earth with your songs of gratitude.

—CHARLES SPURGEON

WHAT SONGS, POEMS, OR VERSES INSPIRE GRATITUDE IN YOU?

HE IS A WISE MAN WHO DOES NOT GRIEVE FOR THE THINGS WHICH HE HAS NOT,

BUT REJOICES FOR THOSE WHICH HE HAS.

—EPICTETUS

What things do you long for that get in the way of appreciating what you already have? How can you let those things go?

THINK OF A TIME YOU TRULY FELT ALIVE.

HOW DID GRATITUDE PLAY A ROLE?

*We can only be said
to be alive in those moments
when our hearts are conscious
of our treasures.*

—THORNTON WILDER

GRATITUDE CAN TRANSFORM
common days into thanksgivings,
turn routine jobs into joy,
and change ordinary
opportunities into blessings.

—WILLIAM ARTHUR WARD

IS THERE A JOB OR CHORE YOU ALWAYS PUT OFF?

Think of a way to approach it with gratitude.

(For example, "I'm thankful that I have a home to clean.")

CAN YOU SEE THE HOLINESS
IN THOSE THINGS
YOU TAKE FOR GRANTED—
A PAVED ROAD OR A
WASHING MACHINE?
IF YOU CONCENTRATE ON
FINDING WHAT IS GOOD
IN EVERY SITUATION,
YOU WILL DISCOVER
THAT YOUR LIFE WILL SUDDENLY
BE FILLED WITH GRATITUDE,
A FEELING THAT NURTURES THE SOUL.

—RABBI HAROLD KUSHNER

What conveniences do you take for granted?

Take note of these simple blessings as you go through your day.

_____

_____

_____

_____

_____

_____

_____

_____

_____

_____

_____

_____

_____

_____

_____

_____

_____

_____

_____

I feel gratitude in my heart each time I can meet someone and look at his or her smile.

—ELIE WIESEL

WHOSE SMILES ARE YOU
GRATEFUL FOR THIS WEEK?

_____
_____
_____
_____
_____
_____
_____
_____
_____
_____
_____
_____
_____
_____
_____
_____

There is no greater gift
YOU CAN GIVE OR RECEIVE
than to honor your calling.

—OPRAH WINFREY

What is your gift, your calling? Not sure? Think about when you feel most alive and full of purpose and passion, when you feel born to do what you're doing.

Growth itself contains the germ of happiness.

—PEARL S. BUCK

What new discovery or growth in your life has spurred thankfulness? How can you keep that going?

*Gratitude spurs us on
to prove ourselves worthy of
what others have done for us.*

THE SPIRIT OF GRATITUDE
IS A POWERFUL ENERGIZER.

—WILFERD A. PETERSON

WHAT HAS SOMEONE ELSE DONE FOR YOU

that has inspired you to be a better person?

SOMETIMES THE MOST
IMPORTANT THING
IN A WHOLE DAY IS
THE REST WE
TAKE BETWEEN
TWO DEEP BREATHS.

—ETTY HILLESUM

What times and places of rest fill you with gratitude?

How can you visit them more often in your life?

_____

_____

_____

_____

_____

_____

_____

_____

_____

_____

_____

_____

_____

_____

_____

_____

_____

_____

At first dreams seem impossible, then improbable, then inevitable.

—CHRISTOPHER REEVE

WHAT DREAMS HAVE YOU BEEN GIVEN?

How have they blessed you and those around you?

BEING YOUR OWN STORY
MEANS YOU CAN ALWAYS
CHOOSE THE TONE.

—TONI MORRISON

What physical reminders or triggers can you spread throughout your surroundings to help you remember to choose gratitude? (Some examples: photos of loved ones, inspirational quotes, bits of nature.)

WHO IS THAT FRIEND IN YOUR LIFE WHO STANDS WITH YOU THROUGH IT ALL?

What specific traits do you appreciate in that friend?

_____

_____

_____

_____

_____

_____

_____

_____

_____

_____

_____

_____

_____

_____

_____

*It is one of the blessings
of old friends that
you can afford to be
stupid with them.*

—RALPH WALDO EMERSON

DRINK DEEPLY

from

GOOD BOOKS.

—JOHN WOODEN

What books have made a difference in your life?

WHAT PROBLEMS ARE BURDENING YOU?

RELEASE THEM HERE.

_____

_____

_____

_____

_____

_____

_____

_____

_____

_____

_____

_____

_____

_____

_____

_____

_____

_____

_____

Since you have to
be alive to have problems,

be grateful for the
opportunity to have them.

—BERNIE SIEGEL

*Over and over I marvel
at the blessings of my life:*

EACH YEAR HAS GROWN
BETTER THAN THE LAST.

—LAWRENCE WELK

How has the past year brought new blessings?

You cannot do a kindness too soon,

FOR YOU NEVER KNOW HOW SOON IT WILL BE TOO LATE.

—RALPH WALDO EMERSON

What act of gratitude or simple kindness have you been
thinking about carrying out? Make a plan to follow through.

No one who achieves success
DOES SO WITHOUT THE HELP OF OTHERS.
THE WISE AND CONFIDENT ACKNOWLEDGE
THIS HELP WITH GRATITUDE.

—ALFRED NORTH WHITEHEAD

Who has been the most influential teacher in your life?

How can you thank that teacher?

_____

_____

_____

_____

_____

_____

_____

_____

_____

_____

_____

_____

_____

_____

_____

_____

_____

_____

*The only people
with whom you should
try to get even are those
who have helped you.*

—JOHN E. SOUTHARD

Think about the challenging people in your life. Are there surprising ways they have blessed you or gifts they have helped you realize through your interactions?

A sense of blessedness comes from a change of heart, NOT FROM MORE BLESSINGS.

—MASON COOLEY

What heart struggles keep you from living a life full of gratitude? (Some examples: envy, impatience.) How can you focus on releasing them in favor of gratitude?

_____

_____

_____

_____

_____

_____

_____

_____

_____

_____

_____

_____

_____

_____

_____

_____

_____

If you participate in social media, hold the rants and aim to share only the good this week. How does it make you feel? What's the response from others? Not on social media? Do the same in your real-time interactions.

Find
the good
and
praise it.

—ALEX HALEY

THE MOST FORTUNATE
have a wonderful capacity
TO APPRECIATE AGAIN AND AGAIN,
freshly and naively,
THE BASIC GOODS OF LIFE,
with awe, pleasure, wonder,
AND EVEN ECSTASY.

—A. H. MASLOW

Find a gratitude partner.

Share what you're grateful for with each other. If you know each other well enough, you may even be able to add to each other's lists. How did this process help? What plan can you make to share with each other regularly?

This is a wonderful day.

I'VE NEVER SEEN THIS ONE BEFORE.

—MAYA ANGELOU

EACH DAY IS A GIFT.

WHAT MADE THIS DAY DISTINCTLY DIFFERENT
THAT YOU CAN BE THANKFUL FOR?

I am especially glad of
the divine gift of laughter:
it has made the world human
and lovable, despite all its
pain and wrong.

—W. E. B. DU BOIS

What people, things, or experiences bring laughter to your life?

WHEREVER YOU GO
BECOMES A PART OF YOU
somehow.

—ANITA DESAI

What trips or places have you enjoyed visiting the most?

_____

_____

_____

_____

_____

_____

_____

_____

_____

_____

_____

_____

_____

_____

_____

_____

_____

What unexpected gifts have made the greatest impact on your life?

Surprise

IS THE GREATEST GIFT
WHICH LIFE CAN GRANT US.

—BORIS PASTERNAK

THERE IS IN SOULS
A SYMPATHY
WITH SOUNDS.

—WILLIAM COWPER

Listen closely.

What gifts can you hear all around you?

All my life through, the new sights of Nature made me rejoice like a child.

—MARIE CURIE

WHAT SIGHTS MAKE YOU "REJOICE LIKE A CHILD"?

Touch

SEEMS TO BE AS ESSENTIAL AS SUNLIGHT.

—DIANE ACKERMAN

What things you touch and feel bring you delight?

What physical activities are you grateful for?

How can you plan to make sure at least one
is included in your week?

_____

_____

_____

_____

_____

_____

_____

_____

_____

_____

_____

_____

_____

_____

_____

ALL THAT IS IMPORTANT IS THIS
ONE MOMENT IN MOVEMENT.
Make the moment important,
vital, and worth living.
DO NOT LET IT SLIP AWAY
UNNOTICED AND UNUSED.

—MARTHA GRAHAM

Angels live among us.

SOMETIMES THEY HIDE THEIR WINGS,
BUT THERE IS NO DISGUISING THE
PEACE AND HOPE THEY BRING.

—ANONYMOUS

RECALL AT LEAST ONE TIME WHEN A COMPLETE STRANGER HELPED YOU.

Our most treasured family heirloom are our sweet family memories.

—WILLIAM FAULKNER

WHAT TRADITIONS ARE
YOU MOST THANKFUL FOR?

OPPORTUNITIES
ARE LIKE SUNRISES.
IF YOU WAIT TOO LONG,
YOU MISS THEM.

—WILLIAM ARTHUR WARD

What opportunities are you thankful that you seized?

What opportunities are in front of you now
that you can be thankful for?

_____

_____

_____

_____

_____

_____

_____

_____

_____

_____

_____

_____

_____

_____

WHAT RISK ARE YOU
GRATEFUL THAT YOU TOOK?

You get in life what you have the courage to ask for.

—OPRAH WINFREY

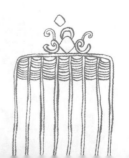

JUST KEEP SAYING
thank you,
FOREVER AND SINCERELY,
FOR AS LONG AS
WE HAVE VOICES.

—ELIZABETH GILBERT

Throughout your day, notice and show gratitude for all the people in your life who serve you—in big or little ways. Note a few and how they serve you here.

WE ALL HAVE BIG CHANGES IN OUR LIVES THAT ARE MORE OR LESS A SECOND CHANCE.

—HARRISON FORD

What second chance are you grateful for?

Sometimes it seems like nothing is working in our lives. Today, take a moment to notice and record all the things that work well for you—from perfectly toasted bread to a car that starts.

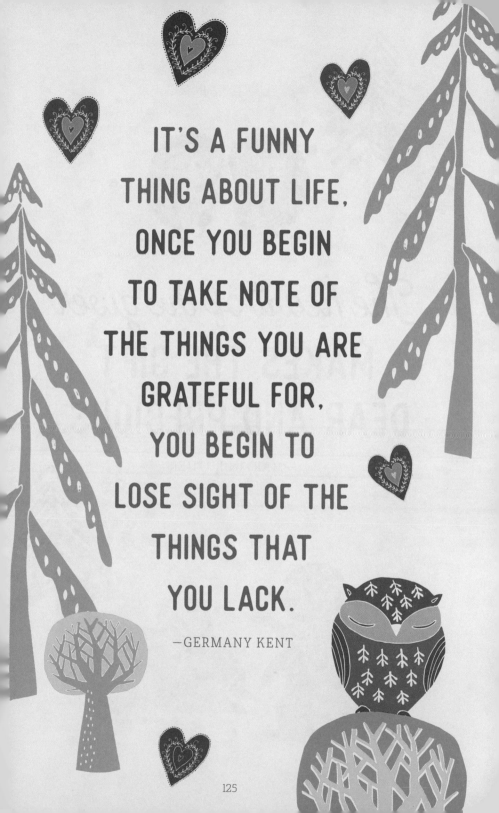

IT'S A FUNNY
THING ABOUT LIFE,
ONCE YOU BEGIN
TO TAKE NOTE OF
THE THINGS YOU ARE
GRATEFUL FOR,
YOU BEGIN TO
LOSE SIGHT OF THE
THINGS THAT
YOU LACK.

—GERMANY KENT

The heart of the giver

MAKES THE GIFT DEAR AND PRECIOUS.

—MARTIN LUTHER

WHAT'S THE BEST GIFT
YOU EVER RECEIVED?

THE SECRET
TO HAVING IT ALL
IS KNOWING
YOU ALREADY DO.

—ANONYMOUS